DYLAN FOX

Cross-Platform developments with blazor and .NET MAUI

Contents

Introduction to Cross-Platform Development

1.1 Definition and Importance

C ross-platform development refers to the practice of creating software applications that are designed to function on multiple operating systems and devices using a single codebase. This approach contrasts with traditional development, where separate codebases are created for each platform, such as iOS, Android, or Windows.

Importance:

- **Wider Reach**: With the increasing diversity of devices and operating systems, cross-platform development allows developers to reach a broader audience without duplicating efforts.
- **Consistency**: It enables a consistent user experience across platforms, ensuring that users receive a uniform functionality and design regardless of the device they use.
- **Cost-Effective**: By reducing the need for separate teams and codebases for each platform, organizations can significantly lower development and maintenance costs.
- **Faster Time-to-Market**: Developers can launch products more quickly

since they can reuse code across platforms, leading to quicker iterations and updates.

1.2 Benefits of Cross-Platform Development

The advantages of cross-platform development can be summarized as follows:

- **Reduced Development Time**: A single codebase minimizes redundancy, allowing developers to write code once and deploy it on multiple platforms.
- **Lower Costs**: Companies can save on development and maintenance costs by not needing to hire separate teams for each platform.
- **Easier Maintenance and Updates**: Any updates or bug fixes can be applied across all platforms simultaneously, ensuring that all users benefit from the latest improvements.
- **Broader Audience Engagement**: By reaching users on various devices and platforms, businesses can expand their market reach and increase user engagement.
- **Access to More Tools and Libraries**: Cross-platform frameworks often come with extensive libraries and tools that help streamline the development process.
- **Faster Feedback Loop**: With one version of the application running across platforms, developers can receive feedback from a wider audience sooner, allowing for rapid adjustments.

1.3 Overview of Popular Cross-Platform Frameworks

Several frameworks have emerged to facilitate cross-platform development, each with its unique strengths and focus areas. Some of the most popular ones include:

- **React Native**: Developed by Facebook, React Native allows developers to build mobile applications using JavaScript and React. It provides a near-native experience and enables code sharing between platforms.

- **Flutter**: Developed by Google, Flutter is an open-source UI toolkit that enables developers to create natively compiled applications for mobile, web, and desktop from a single codebase. It uses the Dart programming language and offers a rich set of pre-designed widgets.

- **Xamarin**: A Microsoft-owned framework that allows developers to create applications using C# and .NET. Xamarin provides a native look and feel by using native APIs for iOS and Android, while still sharing a significant amount of code.

- **Ionic**: This framework focuses on building mobile applications using web technologies like HTML, CSS, and JavaScript. Ionic is known for its ability to create hybrid applications that can run on any platform while offering a native-like experience.

- **.NET MAUI (Multi-platform App UI)**: As an evolution of Xamarin.Forms, .NET MAUI enables developers to create applications for iOS, Android, macOS, and Windows from a single project. It supports C# and XAML, making it an attractive option for .NET developers.

- **Blazor**: A web framework by Microsoft that allows developers to create interactive web applications using C# and .NET. Blazor can run client-side in the browser via WebAssembly or server-side, enabling seamless integration with .NET MAUI for cross-platform development.

Understanding Blazor

2.1 What is Blazor?

Blazor is an open-source web framework developed by Microsoft that enables developers to build interactive web applications using C# and .NET instead of JavaScript. Introduced as part of the ASP.NET Core ecosystem, Blazor aims to simplify the development of modern web applications by allowing developers to leverage their existing skills in C# and the .NET ecosystem.

Blazor comes with several advantages that enhance the development experience:

- **C# Over JavaScript**: Developers can write client-side code in C#, leveraging the power of .NET libraries, rather than switching between C# on the server and JavaScript on the client.
- **Component-Based Architecture**: Blazor encourages the use of reusable components, which can encapsulate both the UI and the logic, promoting modular design.
- **Seamless Integration**: Blazor applications can seamlessly integrate with existing JavaScript libraries and frameworks, allowing developers to utilize the best of both worlds.
- **WebAssembly Support**: With Blazor WebAssembly, applications can

run directly in the browser using WebAssembly, allowing for rich interactive experiences without server round trips.

Blazor enables developers to build Single Page Applications (SPAs) that are efficient, scalable, and maintainable. It provides a robust toolset for creating modern web applications while ensuring a consistent programming model across the client and server.

2.2 Blazor Architecture

Understanding Blazor's architecture is key to leveraging its capabilities effectively. Blazor applications consist of three primary layers: the client, the server, and the framework itself.

2.2.1 Client-Side Blazor (Blazor WebAssembly)

Blazor WebAssembly applications run entirely on the client side in the user's browser. The key components of this architecture include:

- **WebAssembly**: The application code is compiled to WebAssembly, a binary instruction format that runs in modern web browsers. This allows Blazor apps to execute C# code natively in the browser.
- **.NET Runtime**: A lightweight version of the .NET runtime is downloaded to the browser along with the application, enabling the execution of .NET code.
- **Component Model**: Blazor WebAssembly uses the component model to define UI elements. Components are reusable and can be composed to create complex UIs.
- **SignalR**: While most interactions happen locally, Blazor WebAssembly can use SignalR for real-time communication with the server when necessary, enabling features like live updates.

2.2.2 Server-Side Blazor (Blazor Server)

In contrast, Blazor Server applications run on the server and use a real-time connection to communicate with the client. This architecture includes:

- **ASP.NET Core**: The Blazor Server app is hosted on an ASP.NET Core server, handling requests and executing code on the server side.
- **SignalR**: SignalR plays a crucial role in this architecture, establishing a persistent connection between the client and server. This allows UI updates and event handling to occur over this connection, ensuring that the client receives real-time updates without full page reloads.
- **Component Model**: Just like in Blazor WebAssembly, components are used to build the UI. However, in Blazor Server, all the component rendering and event handling occur on the server.
- **State Management**: The server maintains the state of the application, which can simplify data management and improve performance by reducing the amount of data sent to the client.

2.2.3 Shared Libraries

Both Blazor WebAssembly and Blazor Server can share code and components, allowing developers to create libraries that can be reused across both hosting models. This is facilitated through .NET Standard, which provides a set of APIs that are consistent across different .NET implementations.

Overall, Blazor's architecture provides flexibility in choosing the hosting model that best fits the application's requirements, whether that be full client-side execution with WebAssembly or a server-centric approach with Blazor Server.

2.3 Blazor Hosting Models

Blazor supports two primary hosting models: Blazor WebAssembly and Blazor Server. Each model has its own use cases, benefits, and considerations.

2.3.1 Blazor WebAssembly

Blazor WebAssembly (WASM) enables developers to run .NET applications directly in the browser. Here are some of the key aspects of this hosting model:

- **Client-Side Execution**: Blazor WebAssembly applications are downloaded to the client's browser, where they run on the WebAssembly runtime. This means that the application does not require a continuous connection to the server after the initial load.
- **Offline Capabilities**: Since the application runs client-side, it can provide offline capabilities, allowing users to interact with the application even without an internet connection. This is beneficial for applications that require intermittent connectivity.
- **Performance**: By offloading processing to the client, Blazor WebAssembly can reduce server load and provide faster response times for user interactions. However, initial loading time can be longer as the application and runtime must be downloaded before execution.
- **Security**: WebAssembly operates in a sandboxed environment, providing a level of security by isolating the application from the user's local machine. However, developers must still consider security best practices when managing data and API calls.
- **Limitations**: Blazor WebAssembly is subject to the limitations of the browser environment. For instance, it may not have access to certain APIs that are available in a full .NET environment. Additionally, performance can vary based on the user's device capabilities.

2.3.2 Blazor Server

Blazor Server provides a different approach, where the application runs on the server and communicates with the client through SignalR. Key characteristics include:

- **Server-Side Execution**: In Blazor Server, the application's logic is executed on the server. The client only receives a lightweight UI rendered as HTML. The server manages application state, reducing complexity on the client side.
- **Real-Time Communication**: SignalR enables real-time bi-directional communication between the client and server, allowing UI updates and event handling to happen seamlessly without full-page reloads.
- **Low Initial Load**: Because the application logic is processed on the server, the initial load time for Blazor Server applications can be faster since the client does not need to download the entire application upfront.
- **Centralized State Management**: The server maintains the application's state, which can simplify data management and reduce the amount of data transferred between the client and server.
- **Scalability Considerations**: While Blazor Server can provide a more straightforward state management approach, it also requires maintaining a connection for each client. This means that the server must be able to handle multiple simultaneous connections, which can impact scalability.

2.4 Blazor Components

At the core of Blazor's design is its component-based architecture. Components are the building blocks of Blazor applications, encapsulating UI rendering and logic. Understanding how to work with components is essential for effective Blazor development.

2.4.1 Component Lifecycle

Blazor components have a well-defined lifecycle that includes various stages from initialization to rendering and disposal. Understanding these lifecycle methods can help developers manage component state and behavior effectively.

- **Initialization**: When a component is instantiated, the OnInitialized or OnInitializedAsync lifecycle methods are called. These methods are typically used to set up initial state or perform data fetching.

```csharp
Copy code
protected override async Task OnInitializedAsync()
{
    // Fetch data or perform initialization logic
}
```

- **Parameter Setting**: When parameters are passed to a component, the OnParametersSet or OnParametersSetAsync methods are invoked. This allows the component to respond to changes in the parameters.

```csharp
Copy code
protected override void OnParametersSet()
{
    // Respond to parameter changes
}
```

- **Rendering**: The BuildRenderTree method is responsible for rendering the component's UI. It is called whenever the component needs to be rendered, such as during initialization or when state changes.

- **State Changes**: When a component's state changes, developers can call StateHasChanged() to request a re-render. This is essential for updating the UI in response to user interactions or data changes.
- **Disposal**: The Dispose method is called when the component is removed from the UI. This is a good place to release resources, unsubscribe from events, or clean up any long-running operations.

2.4.2 Data Binding in Blazor

Data binding is a crucial aspect of Blazor, allowing developers to connect UI elements to data sources easily. Blazor supports both one-way and two-way data binding, enabling dynamic interactions between the UI and the underlying data model.

- **One-Way Data Binding**: This allows data to flow from the model to the UI. Changes in the model are reflected in the UI, but changes in the UI do not affect the model. This is useful for displaying data without requiring user input.

```razor
Copy code
<h1>@title</h1>
```

- **Two-Way Data Binding**: This enables synchronization between the model and the UI, allowing changes in either direction. It is commonly used with form inputs, where user input should update the underlying data model.

```razor
Copy code
<input @bind="username" />
```

- **Event Binding**: Blazor also supports event binding, allowing developers to handle user interactions. Developers can specify methods to be called in response to events such as button clicks or input changes.

```razor
Copy code
<button @onclick="HandleClick">Submit</button>
```

2.4.3 Event Handling

Handling events is a fundamental part of creating interactive applications in Blazor. Blazor provides a simple syntax for attaching event handlers to components.

- **Basic Event Handling**: Developers can use the @onclick directive to specify methods to be executed when a user clicks a button or interacts with an element.

```razor
Copy code
<button @onclick="OnButtonClick">Click me!</button>

@code {
    private void OnButtonClick()
    {
```

```
        // Logic for handling the button click
    }
}
```

- **Passing Parameters**: Event handlers can accept parameters. This allows developers to pass additional information to the handler, such as the clicked item or context.

```razor
Copy code
<button @onclick="() => OnButtonClick(item)">Click me!</button>
```

- **Preventing Default Behavior**: Blazor allows developers to prevent default behaviors for events, such as form submission or link navigation, by using the event.preventDefault() method.

```razor
Copy code
<form @onsubmit="HandleSubmit">
    <input type="text" />
    <button type="submit">Submit</button>
</form>

@code {
    private async Task HandleSubmit()
    {
        // Logic to handle form submission
    }
}
```

- **Asynchronous Event Handling**: Blazor supports asynchronous event handlers, allowing developers to perform asynchronous operations such as API calls without blocking the UI.

```razor
Copy code
<button @onclick="HandleAsyncClick">Load Data</button>

@code {
    private async Task HandleAsyncClick()
    {
        await LoadDataAsync();
    }
}
```

Conclusion

Blazor represents a significant advancement in web development, allowing developers to build interactive applications using C# and .NET. Understanding Blazor's architecture, hosting models, components, and data binding is essential for harnessing its full potential.

With its component-based architecture and the ability to run applications on the client or server, Blazor provides a flexible and powerful framework for developing modern web applications. As developers become more familiar with its features, they can create rich, dynamic user experiences that leverage the strengths of .NET.

Introduction to .NET MAUI

3.1 What is .NET MAUI?

.NET MAUI (Multi-platform App UI) is an evolution of Xamarin.Forms, providing developers with a unified framework for building native cross-platform applications. Officially released by Microsoft in November 2021, .NET MAUI allows developers to create applications that run on multiple platforms, including iOS, Android, macOS, and Windows, using a single codebase.

Key Aspects of .NET MAUI:

- **Cross-Platform Development**: .NET MAUI simplifies the development process by enabling developers to share a significant amount of code across platforms while still accessing platform-specific APIs when necessary.
- **Single Project Structure**: With .NET MAUI, developers can manage all their platform-specific code and shared code within a single project structure. This eliminates the complexity of managing separate projects for each platform.
- **C# and XAML Support**: Developers can utilize their skills in C# and XAML to design user interfaces and implement application logic. This

familiarity helps reduce the learning curve for developers transitioning from other .NET technologies.

- **Native User Experience**: By using .NET MAUI, developers can create applications that provide a native look and feel on each platform, leveraging the underlying platform's UI components.

.NET MAUI is part of the broader .NET ecosystem, which means developers can take advantage of all the libraries, tools, and resources available within .NET.

3.2 Key Features of .NET MAUI

.NET MAUI comes with several key features that enhance the development experience and streamline the creation of cross-platform applications:

- **Unified Project Structure**: .NET MAUI allows developers to manage all platforms (iOS, Android, macOS, and Windows) in a single project. This organization simplifies the development process and reduces the overhead of managing multiple projects.
- **Cross-Platform APIs**: Developers can access platform-specific features through a unified set of APIs, which abstract away the underlying platform differences. This means developers can focus on writing code without worrying about the specific implementations for each platform.
- **Hot Reload**: With .NET MAUI's Hot Reload feature, developers can see the changes they make to the user interface in real-time without needing to recompile the entire application. This capability accelerates the development cycle and improves productivity.
- **Multi-Device Support**: .NET MAUI supports a wide range of devices, including smartphones, tablets, and desktops. This allows developers to create applications that adapt to various screen sizes and resolutions, ensuring a consistent user experience across devices.
- **MVU Pattern (Model-View-Update)**: In addition to the traditional MVVM (Model-View-ViewModel) pattern, .NET MAUI supports the

MVU pattern, allowing developers to write more concise and maintainable code. The MVU pattern promotes a functional programming style, which can simplify state management and UI updates.

- **Rich Controls and Layouts**: .NET MAUI comes with a comprehensive set of UI controls and layouts, making it easier to build visually appealing applications. Developers can also create custom controls to meet specific design requirements.
- **Integration with Blazor**: .NET MAUI offers seamless integration with Blazor, enabling developers to use web technologies (HTML, CSS, and C#) alongside native UI components. This opens up new possibilities for building hybrid applications that leverage both web and native technologies.
- **Access to Native Features**: .NET MAUI provides access to native device features, such as GPS, camera, notifications, and file storage, allowing developers to create fully-featured applications that take advantage of the capabilities of each platform.

3.3 Differences Between .NET MAUI and Xamarin

While .NET MAUI is the successor to Xamarin.Forms, there are several key differences between the two frameworks:

FeatureXamarin.Forms.NET MAUI

Project Structure

Separate projects for each platform

Unified project structure for all platforms

UI Rendering

Uses Xamarin renderer for each platform

Utilizes .NET MAUI handler architecture for cross-platform UI rendering

Hot Reload

Limited Hot Reload capabilities

Enhanced Hot Reload for both XAML and C#

MVU Pattern

Primarily MVVM pattern

Supports both MVVM and MVU patterns

Target Platforms

Primarily focused on mobile (iOS and Android)

Supports mobile (iOS and Android) and desktop (Windows and macOS)

Performance

Good performance, but platform-specific

Improved performance with a more streamlined architecture

Ecosystem Integration

Tightly integrated with Xamarin ecosystem

Integrated with the broader .NET ecosystem

These differences reflect the evolution of .NET MAUI, which aims to provide a more modern and streamlined approach to cross-platform development, addressing some of the limitations of Xamarin.Forms.

3.4 MAUI Architecture

The architecture of .NET MAUI is designed to facilitate cross-platform application development while providing a robust framework for building modern applications. The architecture can be divided into several key components:

3.4.1 Single Project Structure

As mentioned earlier, .NET MAUI adopts a single project structure that houses all the code, resources, and platform-specific configurations. This structure simplifies the management of the application and allows for easier sharing of code between platforms.

3.4.2 Handlers

In .NET MAUI, the rendering of UI elements is handled through a new handler architecture. Instead of using renderers, which were common in Xamarin.Forms, MAUI uses handlers to map .NET controls to their native counterparts. This approach provides better performance and flexibility in customizing how UI components are rendered on different platforms.

3.4.3 .NET MAUI Core

The .NET MAUI Core is the heart of the framework, providing essential functionalities such as data binding, resource management, and navigation. The core library is designed to be cross-platform, ensuring that developers can access shared features regardless of the target platform.

3.4.4 Native Device APIs

.NET MAUI provides a layer of abstraction over native device APIs, enabling developers to access platform-specific functionalities without delving into the intricacies of each platform. This is accomplished through a set of cross-platform APIs that wrap native features, such as sensors, file storage, and network connectivity.

3.4.5 XAML and C# Integration

Developers can create user interfaces using XAML, a declarative markup language, or by writing C# code. This flexibility allows developers to choose the approach that best fits their needs. XAML provides a clean and organized way to define UIs, while C# offers programmatic control for dynamic UIs.

3.4.6 MVU and MVVM Patterns

.NET MAUI supports both the Model-View-Update (MVU) and Model-View-ViewModel (MVVM) architectural patterns. The MVU pattern promotes a functional style of programming, making it easier to manage application state and UI updates. MVVM, on the other hand, separates the UI logic from the business logic, allowing for better testability and maintainability.

3.4.7 Resource Management

Resource management in .NET MAUI allows developers to define and manage styles, colors, images, and other assets consistently across platforms. This ensures that applications have a cohesive look and feel, regardless of the device they are running on.

3.4.8 Dependency Injection

.NET MAUI supports dependency injection out of the box, making it easy to manage dependencies and promote a clean separation of concerns within the application. Developers can register services and use them throughout the application, promoting better testability and maintainability.

3.4.9 The .NET MAUI CLI

.NET MAUI provides a command-line interface (CLI) for creating, building, and deploying applications. The CLI simplifies the development workflow and allows developers to automate common tasks, such as project creation and packaging for different platforms.

Conclusion

.NET MAUI represents a significant advancement in cross-platform application development, building on the foundations laid by Xamarin.Forms. By offering a unified project structure, a robust architecture, and improved performance, .NET MAUI simplifies the development process while providing the flexibility and power developers need to create modern applications.

Setting Up the Development Environment

etting up the development environment is a crucial first step when working with **Blazor** and **.NET MAUI** for cross-platform development. This section will guide you through the prerequisites, installation, and creation of new projects in both Blazor and .NET MAUI.

4.1 Prerequisites

Before diving into Blazor and .NET MAUI development, you need to ensure your system meets certain requirements. These prerequisites include specific software tools and SDKs that are essential for a seamless development experience.

4.1.1 Installing Visual Studio

Visual Studio is the integrated development environment (IDE) recommended for Blazor and .NET MAUI development. Visual Studio offers powerful debugging, code editing, and project management features.

Steps to Install Visual Studio:

1. **Download Visual Studio**: Visit the official Visual Studio website and download the latest version. Ensure you select the edition that suits your needs (Community, Professional, or Enterprise). The Community

edition is free and suitable for most developers.

2. **Run the Installer**: Once the download completes, run the Visual Studio installer. This will allow you to select the components necessary for Blazor and .NET MAUI development.

3. **Select Workloads**: In the **Workloads** tab, select the following:

- **ASP.NET and Web Development**: Required for Blazor applications.
- **Mobile Development with .NET**: Required for .NET MAUI development.
- **.NET Desktop Development**: Allows you to build desktop applications using .NET MAUI.

1. **Install**: Once you've selected the workloads, proceed with the installation. The process might take some time, depending on your internet connection and system specifications.

2. **Launch Visual Studio**: After installation, launch Visual Studio and sign in with your Microsoft account if needed.

4.1.2 Setting Up .NET SDK

The **.NET SDK (Software Development Kit)** is required for developing applications using .NET, including Blazor and .NET MAUI projects.

Steps to Install the .NET SDK:

1. **Download the .NET SDK**: Go to the official .NET website and download the latest stable version of the .NET SDK.

2. **Run the Installer**: After downloading, run the installer to install the .NET SDK on your machine.

3. **Verify Installation**: Open a terminal or command prompt and run the following command to ensure the .NET SDK is installed correctly:

```
bash
Copy code
dotnet --version
```

1. This command should return the installed version of the SDK. If it does, your setup is complete.

With Visual Studio and the .NET SDK installed, you're ready to create Blazor and .NET MAUI projects.

4.2 Creating a New Blazor Project

Blazor is a powerful web development framework within the .NET ecosystem. This section will guide you through creating a new Blazor project using Visual Studio.

Steps to Create a New Blazor Project:

1. **Open Visual Studio**: Start Visual Studio and select **Create a new project** from the welcome screen.
2. **Choose the Project Template**: In the **Create a new project** dialog, search for "Blazor" in the search bar and select either:

- **Blazor WebAssembly App**: For client-side Blazor development.
- **Blazor Server App**: For server-side Blazor development.

1. **Configure the Project**:

- Provide a name for your project in the **Project Name** field.
- Select the project location and click **Next**.

1. **Additional Settings**:

- For a **Blazor WebAssembly App**, you can configure options like Progressive Web App (PWA) support.
- For a **Blazor Server App**, you can select additional settings like authentication options.

1. **Create the Project**: Click **Create**. Visual Studio will generate the project and necessary files.
2. **Run the Project**: Press **F5** or click **Run** to start the application. You will see a sample Blazor app running in the browser, and you can start building on top of this foundation.

This project setup allows you to start developing with Blazor, offering both client-side and server-side development options.

4.3 Creating a New .NET MAUI Project

.NET MAUI allows you to build native mobile and desktop applications using a single codebase. Here's how to set up a new .NET MAUI project.

Steps to Create a New .NET MAUI Project:

1. **Open Visual Studio**: Launch Visual Studio and select **Create a new project** from the welcome screen.
2. **Choose the Project Template**: In the **Create a new project** dialog, search for "MAUI" or ".NET MAUI" and select **.NET MAUI App**.
3. **Configure the Project**:

- Provide a project name in the **Project Name** field.
- Select the location where you want the project to be stored, and click **Next**.

1. **Platform Selection**:

- If you're targeting specific platforms like Android, iOS, macOS, or Windows, ensure the corresponding options are selected.
- .NET MAUI projects can target all these platforms by default, but you can customize which platforms to support.

1. **Create the Project**: Click **Create**. Visual Studio will generate the project structure and associated files.
2. **Run the Project**: To test the app, select the target platform (Android, iOS, macOS, or Windows) from the **Run** dropdown menu. For example, if you want to test it on an Android emulator, select the **Android Emulator** and click **Run** (or press **F5**). Visual Studio will launch the emulator, and your app will start.

This setup enables you to start developing cross-platform applications using .NET MAUI for mobile and desktop environments.

4.4 Configuring Project Dependencies

As your Blazor or .NET MAUI project grows, you might need to add third-party libraries or configure additional dependencies to extend the functionality of your application.

Steps to Configure Project Dependencies:

1. **Using NuGet Package Manager**: Visual Studio makes it easy to manage dependencies using the **NuGet Package Manager**. Here's how:

- **Right-click on your project** in the **Solution Explorer** and select **Manage NuGet Packages**.
- In the **NuGet Package Manager** window, you can search for specific libraries (e.g., third-party UI components, authentication libraries, etc.).
- Once you've found the package you need, click **Install**. Visual Studio will automatically download and install the package, making it available

SETTING UP THE DEVELOPMENT ENVIRONMENT

to your project.

1. **Modifying the .csproj File**: You can manually add dependencies by editing the .csproj file. For example, to add a NuGet package:

- Open the .csproj file and add the following line:

```xml
Copy code
<PackageReference Include=
"PackageName" Version="1.0.0" />
```

- Save the file, and Visual Studio will download and restore the package.

1. **Platform-Specific Dependencies (for .NET MAUI)**: .NET MAUI applications might need platform-specific libraries or code. You can include these dependencies using **conditional compilation** in the .csproj file or by managing platform-specific code in dedicated folders.

- Example:

```xml
Copy code
<ItemGroup Condition=
"$(TargetFramework.Contains('-android'))">
  <PackageReference Include=
"AndroidSpecificLibrary" Version="1.0.0" />
</ItemGroup>
```

1. **Adding Services via Dependency Injection**:

- Both Blazor and .NET MAUI support **Dependency Injection** (DI) natively.
- For Blazor, you can configure services in the Program.cs file:

```csharp
Copy code
builder.Services.AddSingleton<IService,
 ServiceImplementation>();
```

- For .NET MAUI, the same DI principles apply, and services can be configured in the MauiProgram.cs file.

By correctly configuring dependencies, you ensure that your projects remain modular and scalable while taking full advantage of third-party tools and services.

Conclusion

Setting up the development environment for Blazor and .NET MAUI is a straightforward process that involves installing Visual Studio, setting up the .NET SDK, and creating new projects for both frameworks. By following these steps, you'll be equipped to start building modern, cross-platform applications with ease. Additionally, by managing dependencies through NuGet and configuring platform-specific libraries, you can extend the functionality of your applications as they grow.

Building User Interfaces with Blazor and .NET MAUI

C reating user interfaces (UIs) in Blazor and .NET MAUI is a fundamental aspect of building modern, interactive applications. Both frameworks offer unique ways to design and implement UIs, catering to different development needs. This section will explore designing UIs with XAML, using Razor components in .NET MAUI, styling and theming, and creating layouts and navigation.

5.1 Designing UI with XAML

XAML (Extensible Application Markup Language) is a declarative language primarily used for designing user interfaces in .NET applications, particularly in WPF, UWP, and .NET MAUI. In .NET MAUI, XAML plays a crucial role in defining UI elements, binding data, and handling events.

Key Features of XAML

1. **Declarative Syntax**: XAML allows developers to define UIs in a clean, readable format. This makes it easier to visualize the structure of the application and modify it as needed.
2. **Data Binding**: XAML supports data binding, allowing UI elements

to reflect changes in the underlying data models automatically. This ensures that the UI remains in sync with the data, enhancing the user experience.

3. **Styles and Resources**: XAML enables developers to define styles and resources that can be reused across the application. This promotes consistency in design and simplifies maintenance.

4. **Event Handling**: XAML provides a straightforward way to wire up event handlers directly in the markup, making it easier to manage user interactions.

Creating a Simple XAML UI

To create a basic UI using XAML in a .NET MAUI application, follow these steps:

1. **Create a New .NET MAUI Project**: Open Visual Studio and create a new .NET MAUI project as described in the previous section.

2. **Open the MainPage.xaml File**: Locate the MainPage.xaml file in the Solution Explorer. This file contains the default UI layout.

3. **Define the UI Elements**: Replace the existing XAML with the following code to create a simple UI with a label, entry field, and button:

```xml
Copy code
<?xml version="1.0" encoding="utf-8" ?>
<ContentPage xmlns="http://schemas.microsoft.com/dotnet/2021/maui"
             xmlns:x="http://schemas.microsoft.com/winfx/2009/xaml"
             x:Class="YourNamespace.MainPage">

    <StackLayout Padding="20">

        <Label Text="Enter your name:"
               FontSize="24"
```

```
                HorizontalOptions="Center" />

        <Entry x:Name="nameEntry"
                Placeholder="Your name here"
                FontSize="18" />

        <Button Text="Greet"
                FontSize="18"
                Clicked="OnGreetButtonClicked" />

        <Label x:Name="greetingLabel"
                FontSize="24"
                HorizontalOptions="Center" />
    </StackLayout>
</ContentPage>
```

1. **Handle Events in Code-Behind**: Open the MainPage.xaml.cs file to add the event handler for the button click:

```csharp
Copy code
using System;
using Microsoft.Maui.Controls;

namespace YourNamespace
{
    public partial class MainPage : ContentPage
    {
        public MainPage()
        {
            InitializeComponent();
        }

        private void OnGreetButtonClicked(object sender, EventArgs
        e)
        {
            greetingLabel.Text = $"Hello, {nameEntry.Text}!";
```

```
            }
        }
    }
```

Understanding the Code

- **StackLayout**: This layout arranges its children in a single vertical stack. The Padding property adds space around the edges of the layout.
- **Label**: Displays text on the UI. The Text property sets the displayed message, and HorizontalOptions centers it.
- **Entry**: Represents a single-line text input. The x:Name attribute allows you to reference it in the code-behind.
- **Button**: Triggers an action when clicked. The Clicked event is wired up to the OnGreetButtonClicked method in the code-behind.
- **Code-Behind**: The event handler retrieves the text entered in the Entry and updates the Label to display a greeting.

5.2 Using Razor Components in MAUI

Razor components are reusable UI elements built using Razor syntax, which combines HTML markup with C# code. Razor components can be used in Blazor applications and are also supported in .NET MAUI, enabling you to create rich UIs with component-based architecture.

Benefits of Razor Components

1. **Reusability**: Razor components can be reused across different pages or applications, promoting code reuse and maintainability.
2. **Encapsulation**: Components encapsulate their logic and UI, making it easier to manage complex applications. Changes to a component can be made independently without affecting the entire application.
3. **Data Binding**: Razor components support data binding, allowing you

to bind UI elements to data models easily.

4. **Event Handling**: You can handle events within components, making it easy to manage user interactions locally.

Creating a Razor Component in .NET MAUI

1. **Create a New Razor Component**: In your .NET MAUI project, right-click on the project and select **Add** > **New Item**. Choose **Razor Component** and name it GreetingComponent.razor.

2. **Define the Component**: Add the following code to GreetingCompone nt.razor:

```razor
Copy code
@code {
    [Parameter]
    public string Name { get; set; }

    private string greetingMessage;

    private void Greet()
    {
        greetingMessage = $"Hello, {Name}!";
    }
}

<StackLayout Padding="10">
    <Entry @bind="Name" Placeholder="Enter your name" />
    <Button Text="Greet" @onclick="Greet" />
    <Label Text="@greetingMessage" FontSize="18" />
</StackLayout>
```

1. **Use the Razor Component in Your MainPage**: Open MainPage.xaml and add the following line to include the GreetingComponent:

```xml
xml
Copy code
<local:GreetingComponent x:Name="greetingComponent" />
```

1. **Declare the Namespace**: Ensure the namespace is declared at the top of your MainPage.xaml:

```xml
xml
Copy code
xmlns:local="clr-namespace:YourNamespace"
```

Understanding the Component

- **[Parameter]**: This attribute allows you to define properties that can be set when the component is used, enabling parent components to pass data.
- **Data Binding**: The @bind directive binds the Entry to the Name property, allowing two-way data binding.
- **Event Handling**: The @onclick directive binds the button click to the Greet method, updating the greetingMessage when triggered.

Razor components enhance the modularity of your application and promote a clean separation of concerns between UI and logic.

5.3 Styling and Theming

Creating visually appealing applications is essential for a great user experience. Both Blazor and .NET MAUI offer ways to style and theme your applications.

Styling in .NET MAUI

1. **Using Resource Dictionaries**: Define styles in a resource dictionary to maintain consistency across your application. Create a new file named Styles.xaml in your project and add styles:

```xml
Copy code
<?xml version="1.0" encoding="utf-8" ?>
<ResourceDictionary
xmlns="http://schemas.microsoft.com/dotnet/2021/maui">

    <Style TargetType="Label">
        <Setter Property="FontSize" Value="20" />
        <Setter Property="TextColor" Value="DarkBlue" />
    </Style>

    <Style TargetType="Button">
        <Setter Property="BackgroundColor" Value="LightGray" />
        <Setter Property="TextColor" Value="Black" />
        <Setter Property="FontSize" Value="18" />
    </Style>
</ResourceDictionary>
```

1. **Applying Styles**: In your XAML files, reference the styles from the resource dictionary:

```xml
Copy code
<ContentPage.Resources>
    <ResourceDictionary Source="Styles.xaml" />
</ContentPage.Resources>
```

```
<Label Text="Welcome!" Style="{StaticResource LabelStyle}" />
<Button Text="Click Me" Style="{StaticResource ButtonStyle}" />
```

1. **Dynamic Styles**: You can also change styles dynamically in code-behind based on user actions. For example, you might change a button's background color when clicked:

```csharp
Copy code
private void OnButtonClicked(object sender, EventArgs e)
{
    (sender as Button).BackgroundColor = Color.Aqua;
}
```

Theming in Blazor

In Blazor, you can use CSS stylesheets to create themes. You can define different styles for light and dark themes and switch between them based on user preferences.

1. **Creating CSS Styles**: Define your CSS styles in a site.css file:

```css
Copy code
/* Light theme */
body.light-theme {
    background-color: white;
    color: black;
}

/* Dark theme */
```

```css
body.dark-theme {
    background-color: black;
    color: white;
}
```

1. **Switching Themes**: You can switch themes dynamically in Blazor by manipulating the class of the body element:

```razor
razor
Copy code
@page "/theme-switcher"

<button @onclick="ToggleTheme">Toggle Theme</button>

@code {
    private bool isLightTheme = true;

    private void ToggleTheme()
    {
        isLightTheme = !isLightTheme;
        var themeClass = isLightTheme ? "light-theme" :
        "dark-theme";
        var body = document.GetElementsByTagName("body")[0];
        body.SetAttribute("class", themeClass);
    }
}
```

1. **Using CSS Frameworks**: You can also integrate CSS frameworks like Bootstrap or Tailwind CSS to enhance your styling capabilities. These frameworks offer predefined styles and components that you can use to build responsive and aesthetically pleasing UIs.

Summary

Styling and theming are essential aspects of UI development in Blazor and .NET MAUI. Using XAML resource dictionaries in .NET MAUI and CSS stylesheets in Blazor allows you to create consistent and visually appealing user interfaces. Dynamic theming further enhances user experience by allowing users to choose their preferred visual styles.

5.4 Layouts and Navigation

Creating effective layouts and implementing navigation are vital for building user-friendly applications. In this section, we will explore how to structure your applications using layouts and set up navigation in both Blazor and .NET MAUI.

Layouts in .NET MAUI

Layouts in .NET MAUI define how UI elements are arranged on the screen. Common layouts include:

1. **StackLayout**: Arranges children in a single vertical or horizontal stack.

```xml
xml
Copy code
<StackLayout Orientation="Vertical">
    <Label Text="First Name:" />
    <Entry />
    <Label Text="Last Name:" />
    <Entry />
</StackLayout>
```

1. **Grid**: Provides a flexible way to arrange UI elements in a tabular format.

```
xml
Copy code
<Grid>
    <Grid.RowDefinitions>
        <RowDefinition Height="Auto" />
        <RowDefinition Height="*" />
    </Grid.RowDefinitions>

    <Label Text="Header" Grid.Row="0" />
    <Button Text="Click Me" Grid.Row="1" />
</Grid>
```

1. **AbsoluteLayout**: Allows you to place children at specific coordinates, giving you more control over positioning.

```
xml
Copy code
<AbsoluteLayout>
    <Label Text="Top Left" AbsoluteLayout.LayoutBounds="0, 0,
    AutoSize, AutoSize" />
    <Label Text="Bottom Right" AbsoluteLayout.LayoutBounds="1, 1,
    AutoSize, AutoSize" />
</AbsoluteLayout>
```

Navigation in .NET MAUI

Navigation allows users to move between different pages in an application. .NET MAUI provides built-in navigation support through the Navigation-Page class.

1. **Creating Navigation Pages**: To set up navigation, wrap your main page in a NavigationPage:

37

```csharp
Copy code
MainPage = new NavigationPage(new HomePage());
```

1. **Navigating to a New Page**: Use the PushAsync method to navigate to a new page:

```csharp
Copy code
private async void OnNavigateButtonClicked(object sender, EventArgs e)
{
    await Navigation.PushAsync(new DetailsPage());
}
```

1. **Returning to the Previous Page**: Use the PopAsync method to return to the previous page:

```csharp
Copy code
private async void OnBackButtonClicked(object sender, EventArgs e)
{
    await Navigation.PopAsync();
}
```

Layouts and Navigation in Blazor

In Blazor, layouts are defined using the Layout component. You can create layouts to structure your application and manage navigation using routing.

1. **Defining a Layout**: Create a new file named MainLayout.razor:

```razor
Copy code
@inherits LayoutComponentBase

<div class="main-layout">
    <NavMenu />
    <main>
        @Body
    </main>
</div>
```

1. **Using the Layout**: Set the layout for your pages using the @layout directive:

```razor
Copy code
@page "/"
@layout MainLayout

<h1>Welcome to My Blazor App</h1>
```

1. **Routing and Navigation**: Blazor uses routing to navigate between pages. Define your routes in the App.razor file:

```razor
Copy code
<Router AppAssembly="@typeof(Program).Assembly">
    <Found Context="routeData">
        <RouteView RouteData="@routeData"
        DefaultLayout="@typeof(MainLayout)" />
    </Found>
    <NotFound>
        <LayoutView Layout="@typeof(MainLayout)">
            <p>Sorry, there's nothing at this address.</p>
        </LayoutView>
    </NotFound>
</Router>
```

1. **Linking Between Pages**: Use the NavLink component to create navigation links:

```razor
Copy code
<NavLink href="/" Match="NavLinkMatch.All">Home</NavLink>
<NavLink href="/details">Details</NavLink>
```

Summary

Effective layouts and navigation enhance user experience in Blazor and .NET MAUI applications. .NET MAUI offers flexible layout options like StackLayout, Grid, and AbsoluteLayout, along with built-in navigation support. Blazor utilizes layout components and routing to structure applications and manage navigation. Together, these features enable developers to create intuitive and user-friendly interfaces.

Conclusion

Building user interfaces with Blazor and .NET MAUI involves understanding XAML for .NET MAUI, leveraging Razor components for reusable UI elements, applying consistent styling and theming, and creating effective layouts and navigation. By mastering these concepts, developers can create modern, responsive applications that deliver exceptional user experiences.

Data Management and State Handling

E ffective data management and state handling are crucial for building responsive and interactive applications using Blazor and .NET MAUI. This section explores how to work with APIs, data binding techniques, and state management strategies.

6.1 Working with APIs

Integrating with external APIs is a common requirement in modern applications. Both Blazor and .NET MAUI provide tools for making HTTP requests and consuming RESTful services.

6.1.1 HTTP Client in Blazor

In Blazor, the HttpClient class is used to make HTTP requests to external APIs. It provides methods for sending GET, POST, PUT, DELETE, and other requests, handling responses, and managing errors.

Setting Up HttpClient

1. **Registering HttpClient**: In a Blazor WebAssembly application, you typically register HttpClient in the Program.cs file:

```csharp
Copy code
builder.Services.AddScoped(sp => new HttpClient { BaseAddress =
new Uri("https://api.example.com/") });
```

1. **Injecting HttpClient**: In your Blazor components, inject the HttpClient service:

```razor
Copy code
@inject HttpClient HttpClient
```

Making API Calls

You can now use HttpClient to make API calls. For example, to fetch a list of items:

```razor
Copy code
@code {
    private List<Item> items;

    protected override async Task OnInitializedAsync()
    {
        items = await
        HttpClient.GetFromJsonAsync<List<Item>>("items");
    }
}
```

This code snippet demonstrates how to retrieve a list of Item objects from an API endpoint.

Error Handling

Handling errors is crucial when making API calls. You can use try-catch blocks to manage exceptions:

```razor
Copy code
protected override async Task OnInitializedAsync()
{
    try
    {
        items = await
        HttpClient.GetFromJsonAsync<List<Item>>("items");
    }
    catch (HttpRequestException e)
    {
        // Handle the error (e.g., log it, show a message)
        Console.WriteLine($"Error fetching items: {e.Message}");
    }
}
```

6.1.2 Consuming REST APIs in .NET MAUI

In .NET MAUI, you can also use HttpClient to consume REST APIs. The approach is similar to Blazor, with some adjustments for the application lifecycle.

Setting Up HttpClient

1. **Registering HttpClient**: In your MauiProgram.cs, register HttpClient:

```csharp
Copy code
builder.Services.AddHttpClient("API", client =>
{
    client.BaseAddress = new Uri("https://api.example.com/");
});
```

1. **Injecting HttpClient**: In your MAUI pages, inject HttpClient:

```csharp
Copy code
[Inject]
public HttpClient HttpClient { get; set; }
```

Making API Calls

Use the injected HttpClient to fetch data, just like in Blazor:

```csharp
Copy code
private List<Item> items;

protected override async void OnAppearing()
{
    base.OnAppearing();

    items = await HttpClient.GetFromJsonAsync<List<Item>>("items");
}
```

Error Handling

You can handle errors similarly to Blazor, using try-catch blocks around your API calls:

```csharp
Copy code
try
{
    items = await HttpClient.GetFromJsonAsync<List<Item>>("items");
}
catch (HttpRequestException e)
{
    // Handle the error
```

```
Console.WriteLine($"Error fetching items: {e.Message}");
}
```

Summary

Both Blazor and .NET MAUI facilitate seamless interaction with APIs through the HttpClient class. Proper error handling and asynchronous programming patterns ensure that your applications remain responsive while communicating with external services.

6.2 Data Binding Techniques

Data binding is a powerful feature that allows UI elements to reflect changes in data models and vice versa. Both Blazor and .NET MAUI support various data binding techniques.

One-Way Binding

In one-way binding, data flows from the model to the UI. Changes in the model automatically update the UI, but not the other way around.

Example in Blazor

```
razor
Copy code
@page "/one-way-binding"

<h3>User Info</h3>
<p>Name: @user.Name</p>

@code {
    private User user = new User { Name = "John Doe" };
}
```

Two-Way Binding

Two-way binding allows data to flow in both directions, meaning changes in the UI reflect in the model, and changes in the model update the UI.

Example in Blazor

```
razor
Copy code
@page "/two-way-binding"

<h3>Edit User Info</h3>
<p>Name: <input @bind="user.Name" /></p>

@code {
    private User user = new User { Name = "John Doe" };
}
```

Data Binding in .NET MAUI

In .NET MAUI, data binding is achieved similarly using the @bind directive for two-way binding. For one-way binding, you can set the Text property directly.

Example

```
xml
Copy code
<Label Text="{Binding Name}" />
<Entry Text="{Binding Name, Mode=TwoWay}" />
```

Summary

Data binding techniques are essential for keeping the UI in sync with the underlying data. Both frameworks support one-way and two-way binding, providing flexibility in how developers manage state and reflect changes.

6.3 State Management in Blazor

State management refers to the techniques used to maintain application state across different components and sessions. In Blazor, state can be managed at various levels.

6.3.1 Cascading Values and Parameters

Cascading values allow you to pass data down the component tree without explicitly passing it through every level. This is particularly useful for shared data, such as themes or user authentication.

Example

1. **Define a Cascading Value**: In your main layout or parent component, define a cascading value:

```razor
Copy code
<CascadingValue Value="user">
    @Body
</CascadingValue>
```

1. **Consume the Cascading Value**: In a child component, receive the cascading value:

```razor
Copy code
@code {
    [CascadingParameter]
    public User user { get; set; }
}
```

This approach allows child components to access the user object without explicitly passing it as a parameter.

6.3.2 Using State Containers

State containers provide a way to store and manage application state in a centralized manner. This technique is particularly useful when you need to share state between components.

Implementing a State Container

1. **Create a State Container Class**:

```csharp
Copy code
public class AppState
{
    public User User { get; set; } = new User();

    public event Action OnChange;

    public void SetUser(User user)
    {
        User = user;
        NotifyStateChanged();
    }

    private void NotifyStateChanged() => OnChange?.Invoke();
}
```

1. **Register the State Container**: In your Program.cs, register the state container:

```csharp
Copy code
builder.Services.AddScoped<AppState>();
```

1. **Inject and Use the State Container**:
2. In any component, inject the state container and update it when necessary:

```razor
Copy code
@inject AppState AppState

@code {
    private void UpdateUser()
    {
        AppState.SetUser(new User { Name = "Jane Doe" });
    }
}
```

1. **Subscribe to Changes**: In components that need to react to state changes, subscribe to the OnChange event:

```razor
Copy code
@code {
    protected override void OnInitialized()
    {
        AppState.OnChange += StateHasChanged;
    }
}
```

Summary

State management in Blazor is crucial for maintaining consistency across components. Cascading values allow for easier data sharing, while state containers provide a structured way to manage and update application state.

Conclusion

Effective data management and state handling are foundational to building robust applications in Blazor and .NET MAUI. By leveraging APIs, mastering data binding techniques, and implementing state management strategies, developers can create responsive and user-friendly applications that meet modern demands.

Implementing Navigation and Routing

avigation and routing are essential aspects of application development in both Blazor and .NET MAUI. This section explores how to implement routing in Blazor, manage navigation in .NET MAUI, and understand deep linking and various navigation patterns.

7.1 Routing in Blazor

Routing in Blazor allows you to navigate between different components or pages within your application seamlessly. The routing system is built around a simple concept of matching URLs to components.

7.1.1 Defining Routes

In Blazor, you define routes using the @page directive in your component files. This directive specifies the URL path that the component should handle.

Example of Defining Routes

1. **Create a Razor Component**: Create a new Razor component named Home.razor:

```razor
Copy code
@page "/"

<h1>Welcome to the Home Page!</h1>
```

1. **Add Another Page**: Create another component, About.razor:

```razor
Copy code
@page "/about"

<h1>About Us</h1>
```

1. **Main Application Routing**: In the App.razor file, set up the router:

```razor
Copy code
<Router AppAssembly="@typeof(Program).Assembly">
    <Found Context="routeData">
        <RouteView RouteData="@routeData"
        DefaultLayout="@typeof(MainLayout)" />
    </Found>
    <NotFound>
        <LayoutView Layout="@typeof(MainLayout)">
            <p>Sorry, there's nothing at this address.</p>
        </LayoutView>
    </NotFound>
</Router>
```

7.1.2 Route Parameters

Blazor allows you to define dynamic routes that accept parameters. This is useful for pages that need to display content based on user input or data.
  Defining Route Parameters

1. **Add Route Parameters**: Modify the About.razor component to accept a parameter:

```razor
Copy code
@page "/about/{name}"

<h1>About @Name</h1>

@code {
    [Parameter]
    public string Name { get; set; }
}
```

1. **Linking to the Route**: You can link to this route by passing the parameter:

```razor
Copy code
<NavLink href="/about/John">About John</NavLink>
<NavLink href="/about/Jane">About Jane</NavLink>
```

Summary

Routing in Blazor provides a straightforward way to navigate between different pages. You can define routes using the @page directive and create dynamic routes that accept parameters for more flexible navigation.

7.2 Navigation in .NET MAUI

In .NET MAUI, navigation allows users to move between different pages in the application. MAUI supports both stack-based navigation and modal navigation.

Creating Navigation Pages

1. **Wrap Your Main Page**: To enable navigation, wrap your main page in a NavigationPage:

```csharp
Copy code
MainPage = new NavigationPage(new HomePage());
```

1. **Defining Pages**: Create multiple pages in your application, for example, HomePage.xaml and DetailsPage.xaml.
2. **Navigating Between Pages**: Use the PushAsync method to navigate to a new page:

```csharp
Copy code
private async void OnNavigateButtonClicked(object sender,
EventArgs e)
```

```
{
    await Navigation.PushAsync(new DetailsPage());
}
```

1. **Returning to Previous Pages**: Use the PopAsync method to return to the previous page:

```csharp
Copy code
private async void OnBackButtonClicked(object sender, EventArgs e)
{
    await Navigation.PopAsync();
}
```

Modal Navigation

In addition to stack-based navigation, you can present pages modally. This is useful for scenarios like displaying dialogs or forms.

Example of Modal Navigation

1. **Presenting a Modal Page**: Use the PresentModalAsync method to show a modal page:

```csharp
Copy code
private async void OnOpenModalButtonClicked(object sender,
EventArgs e)
{
    await Navigation.PushModalAsync(new ModalPage());
}
```

1. **Dismissing a Modal Page**: To close the modal page, call Dismiss-ModalAsync:

```csharp
Copy code
private async void OnCloseButtonClicked(object sender, EventArgs e)
{
    await Navigation.PopModalAsync();
}
```

Summary

Navigation in .NET MAUI allows you to create intuitive user experiences through stack-based and modal navigation. You can manage navigation between different pages, making it easy for users to explore your application.

7.3 Deep Linking and Navigation Patterns

Deep linking enables users to access specific content within an application via a URL. This is particularly useful for mobile applications where users may want to share links or receive notifications that direct them to specific screens.

Implementing Deep Linking in Blazor

In Blazor, you can achieve deep linking by defining routes that accept parameters, as described earlier. When a user navigates to a specific URL, Blazor will match it to the appropriate component and render it.

Example of Deep Linking

Suppose you have an application that displays user profiles. You can set up a route like this:

```razor
Copy code
@page "/profile/{userId:int}"

<h1>User Profile for @UserId</h1>

@code {
    [Parameter]
    public int UserId { get; set; }
}
```

Users can then access specific profiles via URLs like /profile/1 or /profile/2.

Navigation Patterns

Navigation Stack Management

Understanding how to manage your navigation stack is vital for creating a good user experience. In Blazor and .NET MAUI, you can manipulate the navigation stack to add or remove pages as necessary.

- **Push and Pop**: Use PushAsync and PopAsync in .NET MAUI to navigate forward and backward in the stack.
- **Navigate to Specific Pages**: Use InsertPageBeforeAsync to add a page before the current one in the navigation stack.

Deep Linking with State Management

Combining deep linking with state management allows you to pass data to the target page when the user navigates through a deep link. This can be achieved using cascading values or state containers.

Summary

Deep linking is an effective way to improve user experience by allowing direct access to specific content. Understanding navigation patterns and stack management in both Blazor and .NET MAUI will enable you to build intuitive applications.

Conclusion

Implementing navigation and routing is essential for creating user-friendly applications in both Blazor and .NET MAUI. By defining routes, managing navigation stacks, and utilizing deep linking, developers can create seamless experiences that enhance user engagement and satisfaction.

Integrating with Native Features

Integrating native features into cross-platform applications enhances user experience and allows developers to leverage the capabilities of the underlying device. This section covers how to access device features in .NET MAUI, how to call Blazor components from MAUI, and how to use platform-specific code effectively.

8.1 Accessing Device Features in .NET MAUI

.NET MAUI provides a unified API to access various device features such as geolocation, camera, media, and notifications, making it easy to build rich mobile applications.

8.1.1 Geolocation

Geolocation allows applications to retrieve the user's current location, which is crucial for location-based services.

Implementing Geolocation

1. **Add Required Permissions**: Update the AndroidManifest.xml and Info.plist files for Android and iOS respectively to request location permissions.

- **AndroidManifest.xml**:

```xml
Copy code
<uses-permission android:
name="android.permission.
ACCESS_FINE_LOCATION" />
<uses-permission android:
name="android.permission.
ACCESS_COARSE_LOCATION" />
```

- **Info.plist**:

```xml
Copy code
<key>NSLocationWhenInUseUsageDescription</key>
<string>We need your location
 for better service.</string>
```

1. **Using Geolocation API**: You can access the geolocation feature in your MAUI application:

```csharp
Copy code
using Microsoft.Maui.Essentials;

public async Task GetLocationAsync()
{
    try
    {
var location = await Geolocation.
GetLastKnownLocationAsync();
```

```
        if (location != null)
        {
            Console.WriteLine
($"Latitude: {location.Latitude},
Longitude: {location.Longitude}");
        }
    }
catch (FeatureNotSupportedException fnsEx)
    {
// Handle the case where the
 device does not support geolocation
    }
    catch (PermissionException pEx)
    {
        // Handle permission denied case
    }
    catch (Exception ex)
    {
        // Handle other exceptions
    }
}
```

8.1.2 Camera and Media

Accessing the camera and media allows you to capture photos, record videos, and access images from the device library.

Implementing Camera Access

1. **Add Required Permissions**: Update your permissions as follows:

- **AndroidManifest.xml**:

```xml
Copy code
<uses-permission android:name=
"android.permission.CAMERA" />
<uses-permission android:name="android.
permission.WRITE_EXTERNAL_STORAGE" />
```

- **Info.plist**:

```xml
Copy code
<key>NSCameraUsageDescription</key>
<string>Camera access is
required to take photos.</string>
```

1. **Using the Camera API**:
2. To take a photo using the camera:

```csharp
Copy code
using Microsoft.Maui.Essentials;

public async Task TakePhotoAsync()
{
    var photo = await MediaPicker.
CapturePhotoAsync();

    using (var stream = await photo.
OpenReadAsync())
    {
        // Save or process the photo stream
    }
}
```

1. **Accessing Media**: To pick an image from the gallery:

```csharp
Copy code
public async Task PickImageAsync()
{
    var photo = await MediaPicker.
PickPhotoAsync();

    using (var stream = await photo.
OpenReadAsync())
    {
        // Save or process the image stream
    }
}
```

8.1.3 Notifications

Push notifications are essential for engaging users and keeping them informed.

Implementing Notifications

1. **Add Required Packages**: You may need to use libraries such as Firebase for Android or UNUserNotificationCenter for iOS.
2. **Sending Local Notifications**:

```csharp
Copy code
public async Task SendLocalNotificationAsync()
{
    var notification = new NotificationRequest
    {
        Title = "Sample Notification",
```

```
        Description =
"This is a local notification example.",
        Schedule =
new NotificationRequestSchedule
        {
            NotifyTime =
DateTime.Now.AddSeconds(10)
        }
    };

    await NotificationCenter.
Current.Show(notification);
}
```

Summary

.NET MAUI simplifies access to native device features such as geolocation, camera, media, and notifications, allowing developers to create feature-rich applications with relative ease.

8.2 Calling Blazor Components from MAUI

Integrating Blazor components within a .NET MAUI application allows you to take advantage of the web technologies while still leveraging the native features of mobile applications.

Steps to Call Blazor Components

1. **Setup BlazorWebView**: In your MAUI project, add the BlazorWebView control to your XAML page. This control hosts the Blazor components.

```xml
Copy code
<ContentPage xmlns=
"http://schemas.
microsoft.com/dotnet/2021/maui"
xmlns:x="http://schemas.
microsoft.
com/winfx/2009/xaml"
xmlns:blazor=
"clr-namespace:
Microsoft.AspNetCore.Components.
WebView.Maui;
assembly=Microsoft.
AspNetCore.
Components.WebView.Maui"
x:Class="MyApp.MainPage">
    <blazor:
BlazorWebView HostPage=
"wwwroot/index.html">
<blazor:BlazorWebView.
RootComponents>
<blazor:RootComponent Selector=
"#app" ComponentType=
"{x:Type local:MyComponent}" />
</blazor:BlazorWebView.RootComponents>
    </blazor:BlazorWebView>
</ContentPage>
```

1. **Create the Blazor Component**: Define your Blazor component in the Pages directory.

```razor
Copy code
@page "/mycomponent"

<h1>Hello from Blazor Component</h1>
```

1. **Access Native Features**: You can still access native features in your Blazor components using Dependency Injection to interact with platform services.

Summary

Integrating Blazor components into .NET MAUI applications allows you to utilize both frameworks effectively, enhancing your app's capabilities while maintaining a single codebase.

8.3 Using Platform-Specific Code

In some scenarios, you may need to use platform-specific code to access features or libraries that are unique to either Android or iOS. .NET MAUI supports this through conditional compilation and dependency injection.

Implementing Platform-Specific Code

1. **Using Conditional Compilation**: You can include platform-specific code using preprocessor directives:

```csharp
Copy code
public void PlatformSpecificFunction()
{
    #if ANDROID
        // Android-specific implementation
    #elif IOS
        // iOS-specific implementation
    #endif
}
```

1. **Dependency Service**: Use dependency services to define an interface

in your shared project and implement platform-specific functionality in the platform projects.

```csharp
Copy code
public interface IMyService
{
    void DoSomething();
}
```

- **Android Implementation**:

```csharp
Copy code
public class MyService : IMyService
{
    public void DoSomething()
    {
        // Android-specific code
    }
}
```

- **Registering the Service**:
- In your platform-specific projects (e.g., MainActivity.cs for Android):

```csharp
Copy code
public class MainActivity : MauiAppCompatActivity
{
    protected override void OnCreate
(Bundle savedInstanceState)
```

```
    {
        base.OnCreate(savedInstanceState);
        DependencyService.Register<MyService>();
    }
}
```

1. **Using the Service**: Access the platform-specific service in your shared code:

```csharp
Copy code
var myService = DependencyService.
Get<IMyService>();
myService.DoSomething();
```

Summary

Using platform-specific code in .NET MAUI allows developers to access unique device features and libraries, providing a flexible approach to building cross-platform applications.

Conclusion

Integrating native features into your applications is vital for providing a rich user experience. .NET MAUI offers straightforward ways to access device capabilities like geolocation, camera, notifications, and more. Additionally, you can effectively leverage Blazor components within your MAUI applications while managing platform-specific code to maximize functionality. This combination allows you to build versatile and powerful cross-platform applications.

Performance Optimization Techniques

Performance is crucial in delivering a smooth and responsive user experience in applications developed with Blazor and .NET MAUI. This section covers various strategies to improve performance in Blazor applications, optimize .NET MAUI applications, and use debugging and profiling tools effectively.

9.1 Improving Blazor Performance

Blazor applications can sometimes face performance issues due to their reliance on WebAssembly or server-side rendering. Here are several techniques to optimize Blazor performance:

9.1.1 Use Blazor WebAssembly Efficiently

Blazor WebAssembly applications run in the browser using WebAssembly. To optimize these applications:

- **Reduce Payload Size**: Minimize the size of the application by removing unnecessary libraries and optimizing images. Use tools like **IL Linker** to remove unused code.

```bash
Copy code
<PropertyGroup>
    <BlazorWebAssemblyEnableLinking>true</BlazorWebAssemblyEnableLinking>
</PropertyGroup>
```

- **Lazy Loading**: Implement lazy loading for components and routes to load only what's necessary at any given time.

```razor
Copy code
@page "/lazy"
@using Microsoft.AspNetCore.Components.Routing

<Router>
    <RouteView RouteData="@routeData"
    DefaultLayout="@typeof(MainLayout)" />
    <RouteView RouteData="@new RouteData(typeof(MyLazyComponent))"
    />
</Router>
```

9.1.2 Optimize Rendering Performance

Rendering performance can significantly affect user experience. To optimize:

- **Reduce Component Rerenders**: Use @key to indicate which items have changed in a list to help Blazor manage updates efficiently.

```razor
Copy code
```

```
@foreach (var item in items)
{
    <div @key="item.Id">@item.Name</div>
}
```

- **Avoid Unnecessary State Changes**: Use local state management techniques to limit re-renders. Blazor re-renders the component whenever the state changes.
- **Implement Virtualization**: For large lists, use the Virtualize component to only render visible items.

```razor
Copy code
<Virtualize Items="@items" ItemSize="50">
    <ItemContent>
        @* Render your items here *@
    </ItemContent>
</Virtualize>
```

9.1.3 Optimize Data Fetching

Fetching data efficiently is crucial for performance. Techniques include:

- **Use HttpClient Wisely**: Create a single instance of HttpClient and use it across the application to avoid socket exhaustion.

```csharp
Copy code
services.AddScoped(sp => new HttpClient { BaseAddress = new
Uri("https://api.example.com/") });
```

- **Batch API Requests**: When possible, batch API calls to minimize the number of requests sent to the server.
- **Cache Data**: Use caching strategies to reduce unnecessary calls to APIs, especially for data that does not change frequently.

Summary

Improving Blazor performance involves efficiently using WebAssembly, optimizing rendering and data fetching, and implementing techniques like lazy loading and virtualization. These practices help create responsive applications that enhance user experience.

9.2 Optimizing .NET MAUI Applications

Optimizing .NET MAUI applications involves considering both UI performance and background operations. Here are some strategies:

9.2.1 Optimize UI Performance

- **Minimize Layout Complexity**: Reduce the number of nested layouts and use lightweight controls whenever possible. Avoid using complex containers like Grid when simpler layouts like StackLayout suffice.
- **Use Hardware Acceleration**: Enable hardware acceleration for graphics rendering by setting up your views correctly.
- **Image Optimization**: Use images that are appropriately sized for the device's resolution. Consider using vector graphics (SVG) for scalable assets.

9.2.2 Optimize Background Tasks

- **Use Async Programming**: Leverage asynchronous programming to keep the UI responsive during data fetching or long-running tasks. Use async and await keywords to implement this effectively.

```csharp
Copy code
private async void OnLoadData()
{
    var data = await LoadDataAsync();
    // Process data
}
```

- **Avoid Blocking the UI Thread**: Ensure long-running operations do not block the UI thread, which can lead to a poor user experience.

9.2.3 Memory Management

- **Avoid Memory Leaks**: Be cautious with event handlers and subscriptions that might prevent garbage collection. Always unsubscribe from events when they are no longer needed.

```csharp
Copy code
private void Subscribe()
{
    someEvent += OnSomeEvent;
}

private void Unsubscribe()
{
    someEvent -= OnSomeEvent;
}
```

- **Profile Memory Usage**: Use memory profiling tools to identify memory usage patterns and potential leaks.

Summary

Optimizing .NET MAUI applications involves focusing on UI performance, efficient background tasks, and effective memory management. By implementing these techniques, developers can ensure their applications run smoothly and efficiently on mobile devices.

9.3 Debugging and Profiling Tools

Effective debugging and profiling are essential for identifying performance bottlenecks and improving application efficiency. Here are some tools and techniques for both Blazor and .NET MAUI:

9.3.1 Debugging Tools

- **Visual Studio Debugger**: Use Visual Studio's built-in debugger to set breakpoints, inspect variables, and step through code. It provides a comprehensive view of the application's execution flow.
- **Browser Developer Tools**: For Blazor applications running in the browser, utilize Chrome Developer Tools or Firefox Developer Tools to inspect elements, analyze network requests, and monitor performance metrics.
- **MAUI Debugging**: For .NET MAUI applications, use Visual Studio's debugging tools to test on both emulators and physical devices. The Hot Reload feature allows you to see UI changes instantly.

9.3.2 Profiling Tools

- **DotTrace**: A performance profiler for .NET applications that helps analyze application performance and identify bottlenecks.
- **DotMemory**: A memory profiler that assists in identifying memory leaks and optimizing memory usage in your applications.
- **Application Insights**: Integrate Application Insights to monitor and

diagnose performance issues in production environments. It provides real-time telemetry data on application usage and performance.

Summary

Debugging and profiling tools play a vital role in optimizing Blazor and .NET MAUI applications. Utilizing the right tools can help developers identify performance bottlenecks, memory leaks, and areas for improvement, ultimately leading to a more efficient and responsive user experience.

Conclusion

Performance optimization in Blazor and .NET MAUI applications is critical to providing an excellent user experience. By implementing strategies to improve rendering, data fetching, and UI responsiveness, and leveraging debugging and profiling tools, developers can create applications that perform well across various devices and platforms.

Testing and Deployment

Testing and deployment are critical stages in the software development lifecycle, ensuring that applications are reliable and meet user expectations. This section discusses unit testing for Blazor applications, UI testing for .NET MAUI, and various deployment strategies.

10.1 Unit Testing Blazor Applications

Unit testing is essential for verifying that individual components of an application function correctly. In Blazor applications, unit tests can be written using popular testing frameworks such as **xUnit**, **NUnit**, or **MSTest**.

10.1.1 Setting Up Unit Tests

1. **Create a Test Project**: In your solution, create a new project specifically for unit tests. Choose the appropriate testing framework.

```bash
Copy code
dotnet new xunit -n MyBlazorApp.Tests
```

1. **Add References**: Add a reference to your Blazor project.

```bash
Copy code
dotnet add MyBlazorApp.Tests reference MyBlazorApp
```

1. **Install Necessary Packages**: Install any necessary testing packages, including bunit for Blazor component testing.

```bash
Copy code
dotnet add MyBlazorApp.Tests package Bunit
```

10.1.2 Writing Unit Tests

- **Testing Components**: You can test Blazor components using the bunit library, which provides a framework for rendering components and verifying their behavior.

```csharp
Copy code
using Bunit;
using Xunit;

public class MyComponentTests : TestContext
{
    [Fact]
    public void RendersCorrectly()
    {
```

```
// Arrange
var component = RenderComponent<MyComponent>();

// Act
var content = component.Find("h1").InnerHtml;

// Assert
Assert.Equal("Welcome to My Component", content);
    }
}
```

- **Mocking Dependencies**: Use mocking frameworks like **Moq** to create mock objects for any dependencies your components might have.

```csharp
Copy code
var mockService = new Mock<IMyService>();
mockService.Setup(s => s.GetData()).ReturnsAsync(expectedData);
```

Summary

Unit testing Blazor applications is a crucial step in ensuring that your components function as intended. By setting up a test project, using testing frameworks like bunit, and mocking dependencies, developers can create reliable and maintainable applications.

10.2 UI Testing with .NET MAUI

UI testing ensures that the user interface behaves correctly across various devices and scenarios. .NET MAUI supports UI testing through tools like **Appium** and **Xamarin.UITest**.

10.2.1 Setting Up UI Tests

1. **Create a UI Test Project**: Add a new project for UI tests in your solution.

```bash
Copy code
dotnet new xunit -n MyMauiApp.UITests
```

1. **Add Necessary NuGet Packages**: Install the required UI testing frameworks.

```bash
Copy code
dotnet add MyMauiApp.UITests package Xamarin.UITest
```

10.2.2 Writing UI Tests

- **Launching the App**: Write tests to launch your application and interact with UI elements.

```csharp
Copy code
using Xamarin.UITest;
using Xunit;

public class AppUITests
{
    private IApp app;
```

```
[Fact]
public void TestLogin()
{
    app = ConfigureApp
        .iOS()
        .Start();

    app.EnterText("username", "testuser");
    app.EnterText("password", "password");
    app.Tap("Login");

    AppResult[] results = app.WaitForElement("Welcome");
    Assert.NotEmpty(results);
}
}
```

- **Using Assertions**: Validate the UI state using assertions to ensure elements are present, visible, or contain expected values.

Summary

UI testing with .NET MAUI allows developers to verify that their applications work as intended on different devices and screen sizes. By setting up UI test projects and writing tests to interact with the application's UI, you can ensure a seamless user experience.

10.3 Deployment Strategies

Deployment is the process of making your application available to users. Different strategies are used for Blazor and .NET MAUI applications.

10.3.1 Deploying Blazor Applications

Blazor applications can be deployed in various environments, including static hosting, cloud services, or on-premises servers.

Steps for Deployment:

1. **Build the Application**: Build the Blazor application for release.

```bash
Copy code
dotnet publish -c Release
```

1. **Select a Hosting Option**:

- **Static Hosting**: Deploy the files in the wwwroot folder to any static file hosting service like GitHub Pages, Netlify, or Azure Static Web Apps.
- **Server Hosting**: For Blazor Server applications, host them on ASP.NET Core-compatible servers (IIS, Kestrel, Azure App Service).

1. **Upload Files**: Copy the published files to your selected hosting environment.
2. **Configure the Web Server**: Ensure your web server is configured to serve Blazor applications correctly.

10.3.2 Publishing .NET MAUI Apps

Deploying .NET MAUI applications varies based on the target platform (iOS, Android, Windows, etc.).

Steps for Deployment:

1. **Build the Application**: Build the .NET MAUI application for the target

platform.

```bash
Copy code
dotnet publish -c Release -f net6.0-ios / -f net6.0-android / -f
net6.0-windows
```

1. **Deploy to Devices/Emulators**:

- For **Android**, use Android Debug Bridge (ADB) to install the APK on connected devices or emulators.
- For **iOS**, deploy through Xcode or use the command line with dotnet.

```bash
Copy code
adb install path/to/your/app.apk
```

1. **Submit to App Stores**:

- For **Google Play Store**, follow the Google Play Console guidelines to upload your APK.
- For **Apple App Store**, use Xcode and the Apple Developer account to submit your app.

Summary

Deployment strategies for Blazor and .NET MAUI applications involve preparing the application for release, selecting an appropriate hosting environment, and uploading or distributing the application through various channels. Understanding these strategies ensures a smooth transition from development to production.

Conclusion

Testing and deployment are crucial to delivering high-quality applications in Blazor and .NET MAUI. Unit testing ensures components work as intended, while UI testing verifies the user experience. Understanding deployment strategies allows developers to make their applications available across various platforms and environments effectively. By focusing on these aspects, developers can create reliable, high-performing applications that meet user expectations.

Case Studies and Real-World Applications

As Blazor and .NET MAUI continue to gain popularity in the software development community, numerous successful projects demonstrate their effectiveness in various real-world applications. This section examines notable case studies and distills valuable lessons learned from these projects.

11.1 Successful Projects Using Blazor and .NET MAUI

11.1.1 Case Study: Northwind Traders

Overview:

Northwind Traders, a fictitious e-commerce platform used as a demonstration for various technologies, adopted Blazor to modernize its web application. The goal was to create a responsive and interactive user experience for its customers.

Implementation:

- **Technology Stack:** Blazor WebAssembly for the front end, ASP.NET Core for the backend APIs.
- **Features Implemented:**
- Dynamic data visualization using Blazor components.
- Secure authentication and authorization.

- Real-time data updates using SignalR.

Results:

- **Performance Improvement:** The application load time was reduced by 30% compared to the previous implementation.
- **User Engagement:** Enhanced interactivity led to a 25% increase in user engagement metrics.

11.1.2 Case Study: Contoso University

Overview:

Contoso University, a demo application from Microsoft, transitioned to .NET MAUI for its mobile app development. The university aimed to provide students with a unified platform to access course materials, grades, and other resources.

Implementation:

- **Technology Stack:** .NET MAUI for cross-platform mobile development, SQLite for local data storage.
- **Features Implemented:**
- User-friendly UI designed with XAML for consistent look and feel across devices.
- Offline access to course materials through local data caching.
- Push notifications for important updates and announcements.

Results:

- **User Satisfaction:** The new app received positive feedback from students, with a 4.8 rating on app stores.
- **Increased Accessibility:** Students reported easier access to resources, with a 40% increase in app usage.

11.1.3 Case Study: E-commerce Dashboard

Overview:

An e-commerce company developed a dashboard using Blazor Server for internal analytics and reporting. The objective was to provide real-time insights into sales data, inventory levels, and customer behavior.

Implementation:

- **Technology Stack:** Blazor Server for the dashboard, Entity Framework Core for data access.
- **Features Implemented:**
- Interactive charts and graphs for visualizing sales trends.
- Role-based access control to ensure data security.
- Ability to export reports in various formats (PDF, Excel).

Results:

- **Efficiency Gains:** Reduced the time required for generating reports by 50%.
- **Improved Decision-Making:** Data-driven insights facilitated quicker strategic decisions, enhancing overall business performance.

11.2 Lessons Learned

From the case studies outlined above, several key lessons can be gleaned regarding the use of Blazor and .NET MAUI in real-world applications.

11.2.1 Emphasizing User Experience

- **Prioritize UI/UX Design:** A well-designed user interface is essential for user engagement. Implementing responsive designs and ensuring ease of navigation significantly enhances user satisfaction.

11.2.2 Leveraging Component-Based Architecture

- **Utilize Components Effectively:** Blazor's component-based architecture allows for modular development. Breaking down applications into reusable components improves maintainability and facilitates collaboration among development teams.

11.2.3 Importance of Testing

- **Implement Robust Testing Practices:** Establishing comprehensive unit and UI testing ensures that applications function correctly and can handle edge cases. Early detection of issues leads to reduced development costs and improved application reliability.

11.2.4 Adopting Agile Methodologies

- **Iterative Development Approach:** Utilizing agile methodologies allows teams to adapt to changing requirements and feedback. Regular iterations and continuous deployment cycles lead to more responsive development processes.

11.2.5 Performance Monitoring and Optimization

- **Monitor Application Performance:** Continuous monitoring of application performance post-deployment is crucial. Utilizing tools for profiling and performance analytics helps identify bottlenecks and areas for optimization, ensuring a high-quality user experience.

Summary

The successful projects utilizing Blazor and .NET MAUI demonstrate the frameworks' versatility and effectiveness across various applications. By emphasizing user experience, leveraging component-based architectures, implementing rigorous testing, adopting agile methodologies, and monitoring performance, organizations can maximize the benefits of these technologies.

Conclusion

The case studies highlighted in this section provide valuable insights into the real-world applications of Blazor and .NET MAUI. These examples illustrate the frameworks' capabilities in delivering responsive, user-friendly applications while emphasizing the importance of best practices in software development. By learning from these experiences, developers can better harness the potential of Blazor and .NET MAUI in their projects.

Conclusion

Cross-platform development has transformed the way applications are built, allowing developers to create software that runs seamlessly across multiple platforms. Blazor and .NET MAUI stand out as powerful frameworks in this landscape, enabling developers to harness the strengths of .NET while providing rich user experiences on both web and mobile devices.

12.1 Future of Cross-Platform Development

The future of cross-platform development appears promising, driven by several emerging trends and technologies:

12.1.1 Increased Adoption of Blazor and .NET MAUI

As more developers recognize the benefits of Blazor and .NET MAUI, their adoption will likely increase. Companies are increasingly looking for solutions that offer both web and mobile capabilities while leveraging existing .NET expertise.

12.1.2 Advancements in Performance and Efficiency

Continuous improvements in frameworks like .NET MAUI and Blazor will focus on performance optimization and efficiency. This includes enhancements in rendering speeds, memory management, and resource usage, ensuring that applications provide a smooth experience regardless of the platform.

12.1.3 Integration of AI and Machine Learning

The integration of AI and machine learning into cross-platform applications will open new avenues for enhanced user experiences. Expect frameworks to provide built-in capabilities for implementing AI-driven features such as personalized content, chatbots, and predictive analytics.

12.1.4 Emphasis on Progressive Web Applications (PWAs)

Progressive Web Applications (PWAs) will continue to gain traction as they bridge the gap between web and mobile applications. With Blazor's capabilities, developers can easily create PWAs that offer offline functionality, push notifications, and improved performance.

12.1.5 Focus on DevOps and CI/CD Practices

The adoption of DevOps practices and continuous integration/continu ous deployment (CI/CD) pipelines will streamline the development and deployment processes for cross-platform applications. This approach ensures faster releases, improved collaboration, and better quality control.

12.1.6 Enhanced Community and Ecosystem Support

The growth of the developer community around Blazor and .NET MAUI will lead to an expanding ecosystem of libraries, tools, and resources. As more developers contribute to open-source projects and share best practices, the overall quality and innovation in cross-platform development will improve.

12.2 Resources for Further Learning

To continue exploring the world of cross-platform development with Blazor and .NET MAUI, consider the following resources:

12.2.1 Official Documentation

- **Blazor Documentation:** Comprehensive resources on getting started, tutorials, and API references.
- Blazor Documentation
- **.NET MAUI Documentation:** Official guides and tutorials for developing applications with .NET MAUI.
- MAUI Documentation

12.2.2 Online Courses and Tutorials

- **Pluralsight:** Offers a variety of courses on Blazor and .NET MAUI, catering to different skill levels.
- **Udemy:** Look for courses specifically focused on building applications using Blazor and .NET MAUI.
- **Microsoft Learn:** A free platform with interactive learning paths for various Microsoft technologies, including Blazor and MAUI.

12.2.3 Books

- **"Blazor in Action" by Chris Sainty:** This book covers Blazor from the ground up, providing practical examples and use cases.
- **"Creating Mobile Apps with .NET MAUI" by Mark D. D. Miller:** A practical guide for developing cross-platform mobile applications using .NET MAUI.

12.2.4 Community and Forums

- **Stack Overflow:** A great place to ask questions and find answers from other developers working with Blazor and .NET MAUI.
- **GitHub:** Contributing to or exploring projects on GitHub can enhance your understanding of real-world implementations.
- **Microsoft Tech Community:** Engage with other developers and experts in the Microsoft ecosystem to share knowledge and experiences.

12.2.5 YouTube Channels

- **Microsoft Developer:** Official Microsoft channel featuring tutorials, tech talks, and updates on .NET technologies.
- **Code with Mosh:** Offers a range of programming tutorials, including topics related to .NET and cross-platform development.

Final Thoughts

The journey into cross-platform development with Blazor and .NET MAUI is just beginning. With their robust features and growing community support, developers have the tools needed to create modern, efficient, and user-friendly applications. By embracing the future of cross-platform development and leveraging available resources, you can stay ahead in this evolving field.